MACK WILBERG

REQUIEM

vocal score

MUSIC DEPARTMENT

OXFORD
UNIVERSITY PRESS

OXFORD
UNIVERSITY PRESS

198 Madison Avenue, New York, NY, 10016, USA
Great Clarendon Street, Oxford OX2 6DP, England

Oxford University Press is a department of the University of Oxford.
It furthers the University's aim of excellence in research, scholarship,
and education by publishing worldwide

Oxford New York
Auckland Bangkok Buenos Aires Cape Town Chennai
Dar es Salaam Delhi Hong Kong Istanbul Karachi Kolkata
Kuala Lumpur Madrid Melbourne Mexico City Mumbai Nairobi
São Paulo Shanghai Taipei Tokyo Toronto

First published 2008

3 5 7 9 10 8 6 4 2

ISBN 978-0-19-380454-8

Music origination by Enigma Music Production Services, Amersham, Bucks, UK
Printed in the United States of America on acid-free paper

Contents

Orchestration

3 Flutes (Flute 3 doubles piccolo)
2 Oboes (double 2 English Horns)
2 Clarinets in B♭
2 Bassoons
4 Horns in F
Celeste (Glockenspiel in absence of Celeste)
Harp
Piano
Organ (optional)
Violin 1
Violin 2
Viola
Cello
Double Bass

Duration: 34 minutes

Texts and Translations

1. Requiem aeternam
Introit from Requiem

Requiem aeternam dona eis, Domine
et lux perpetua luceat eis.

*Grant to them eternal rest, O Lord,
and let perpetual light shine upon them.*

2. Kyrie

Kyrie eleison.
Have mercy, hear my
Christe eleison.
Have mercy, hear my cry.

Lord have mercy.

Christ have mercy.

3. I will lift up mine eyes
Psalm 121, adpt.

I will lift up mine eyes unto the hills,
from whence cometh my help.
My help cometh from the Lord,
who made heaven and earth.
He will not suffer thy foot to be moved:
and he that keepeth will not sleep.
Behold, he that keepeth Israel
shall neither slumber or sleep.
The Lord himself is thy keeper:
the Lord is thy defense upon thy right hand;
So that the sun shall not burn thee by day,
neither the moon by night.
The Lord shall preserve thee from all evil:
yea, it is even he that shall keep thy soul.
The Lord shall preserve thy going out,
and thy coming in:
from this time forth for evermore.

4. How lovely is thy dwelling place
Psalm 84:1-5, adpt.

How lovely is thy dwelling place, O Lord, O Lord, of hosts.
My soul longeth, yea, it fainteth for the courts of the Lord,
my heart and my flesh crieth out for the living God.
Yea, the sparrow hath found a house,
and the swallow a nest where she may lay her young,
e'vn thy altars, O Lord of hosts, my King and my God.
Blessed are they that dwell in thy house,
they are ever praising thee.
Blessed are those whose strength is in thee,
They go from strength to strength, appeareth before God.

5. O nata lux
10th-cent. Latin Hymn

O nata lux de lumine,
Jesu, redemptor saeculi
dignare clemens supplicum
laudes preces que sumere.
Qui carne quondam contegi
dignatus es pro perditis,
nos membra confer effici
tui beati corporis.

O Jesus, born light
Redeemer of the world,
mercifully, accept and sanctify
our praises and prayers.
Thou who once was clothed in flesh
for the sake of those who were lost,
O make us Thine,
Thy sons and daughters all.

6. The Lord is my shepherd
Psalm 23, adpt.

The Lord is my shepherd;
therefore can I lack nothing.
He shall feed me in green pastures
and lead me forth beside the waters of comfort.
He shall convert my soul
and bring me forth in the paths of righteousness.
Yea, though I walk through the valley of the shadow of death,
I will fear no evil; thy rod and staff, they comfort me.
Thou shalt prepare a table before me against those that trouble me;
Thou anointed my head with oil, and my cup shall be full.
But thy loving kindness and mercy
shall follow me all the days of my life
and I will dwell in the house of the Lord forever.

7. I am the resurrection and the Life
— Requiem aeternam
John 11:25-26, adpt.
Introit from Requiem

I am the resurrection and the life, saith the Lord.
he that believeth in me, though he were dead, yet shall he live;
and whosoever liveth and believeth in me shall never die.

Requiem aeternam dona eis, Domine: *Grant to them eternal rest, O Lord,*
et lux perpetua luceat eis.   *and let perpetual light shine upon them.*

*In memory of loved ones passed and written for the Mormon Tabernacle Choir
and Orchestra at Temple Square, Craig Jessop, Music Director*

REQUIEM

1. Requiem aeternam*

Introit from Requiem

MACK WILBERG

*This movement was commissioned by the Carnegie Hall Corporation for the Carnegie Hall National High School Choral Festival. The world premiere was given by the festival participants and the Orchestra of St. Luke's conducted by Craig Jessop in the Isaac Stern Auditorium, Carnegie Hall, New York City on March 14, 2006.

A full score and set of parts for an orchestral accompaniment (3 [3+picc].2[2eh].2.2–4.0.0.0–cel/glk–hp.pno.org(opt.)–str) are available on rental from the Publisher.

The Mormon Tabernacle Choir and the Orchestra at Temple Square with Frederica von Stade, mezzo-soprano, and Bryn Terfel, baritone, have recorded this work on the CD *Mack Wilberg: Requiem and Other Choral Works* (SKU4996466).

Printed in the USA

OXFORD UNIVERSITY PRESS, 198 MADISON AVENUE, NEW YORK, NY 10016
Photocopying this copyright material is ILLEGAL.

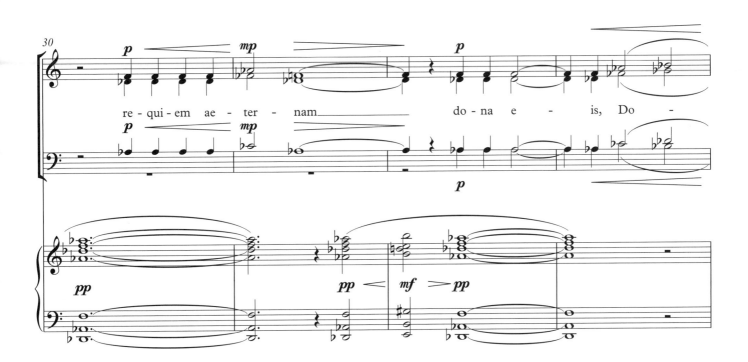

4

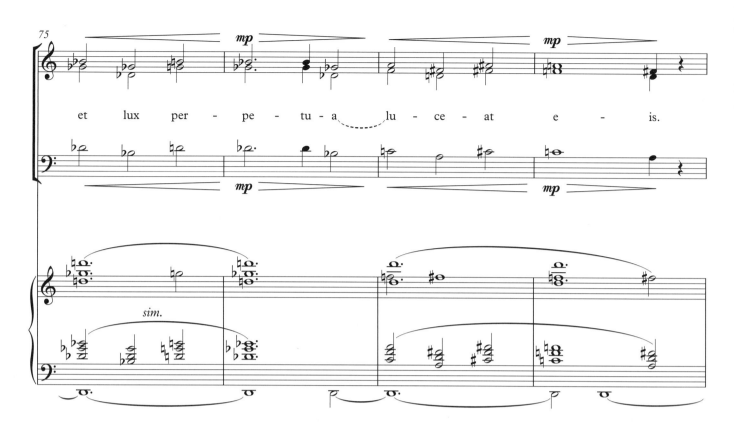

et lux per - pe - tu - a lu - ce - at e - is.

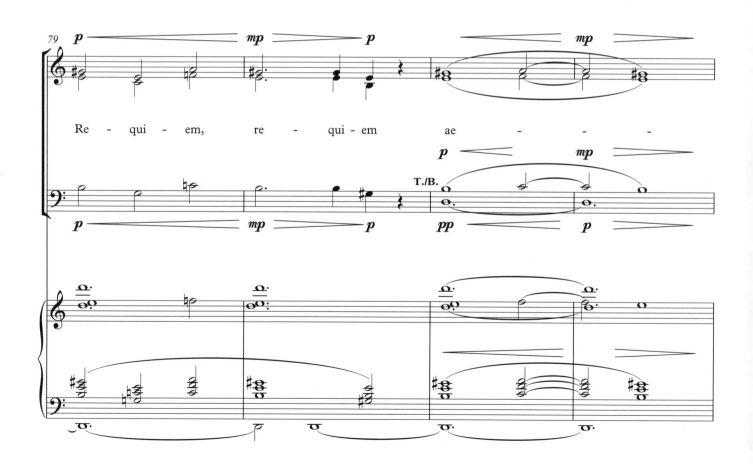

Re - qui - em, re - qui - em ae - - -

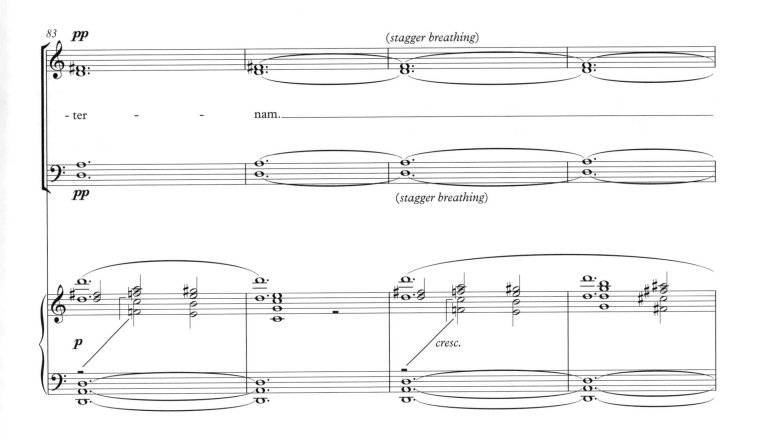

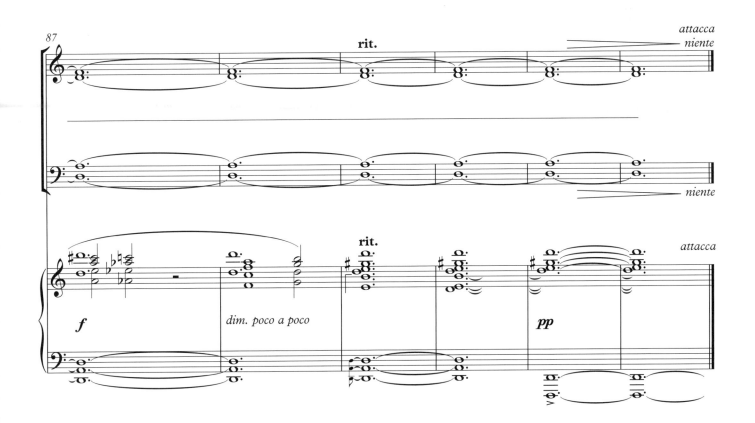

2. Kyrie

Kyrie from Requiem

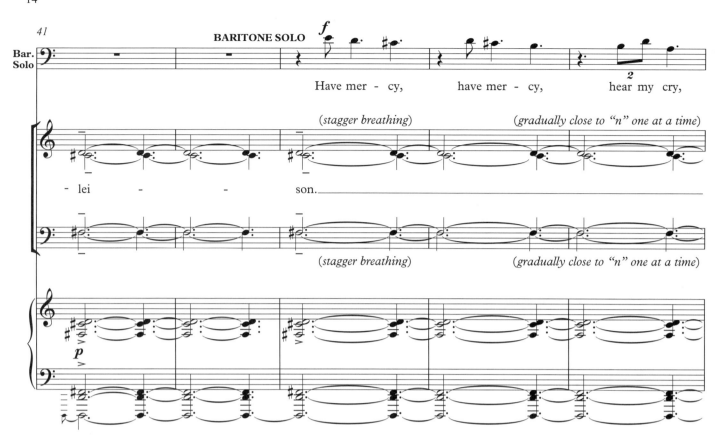

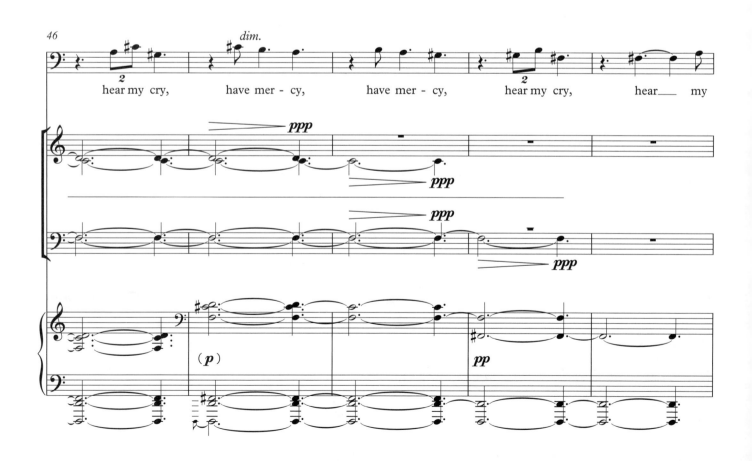

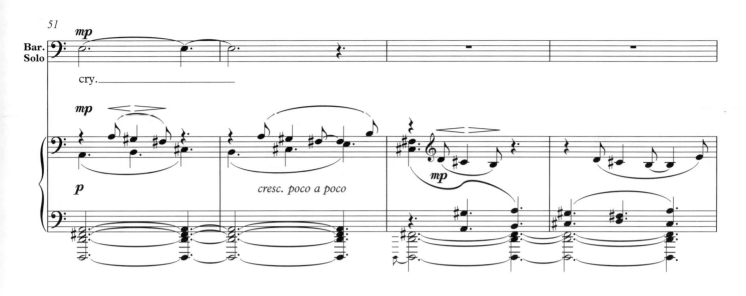

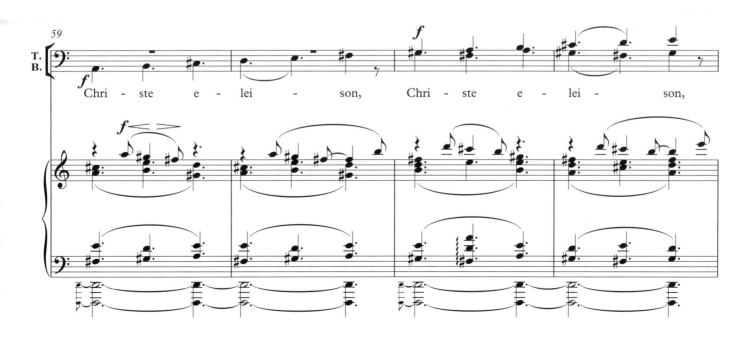

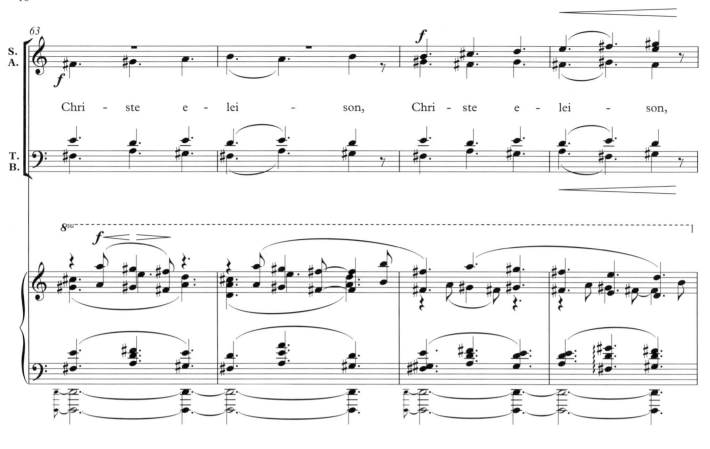

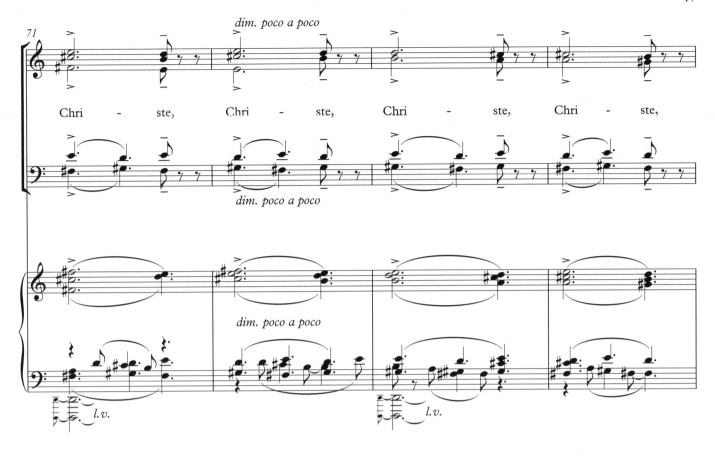

hear my cry, hear my cry.

3. I will lift up mine eyes

Psalm 121, adpt.

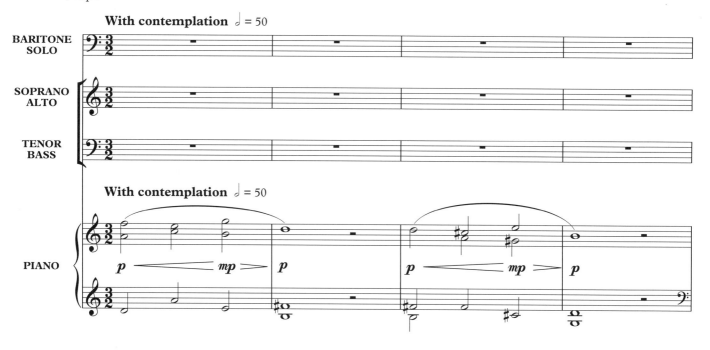

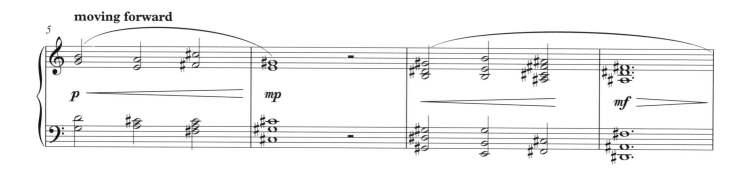

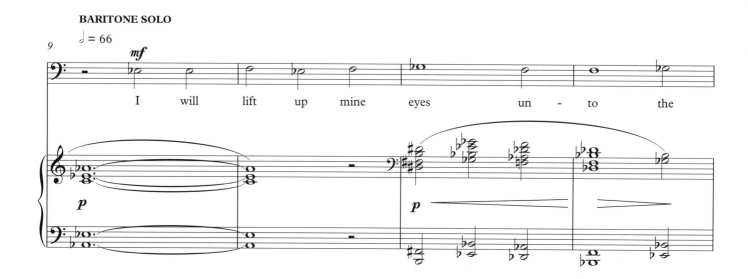

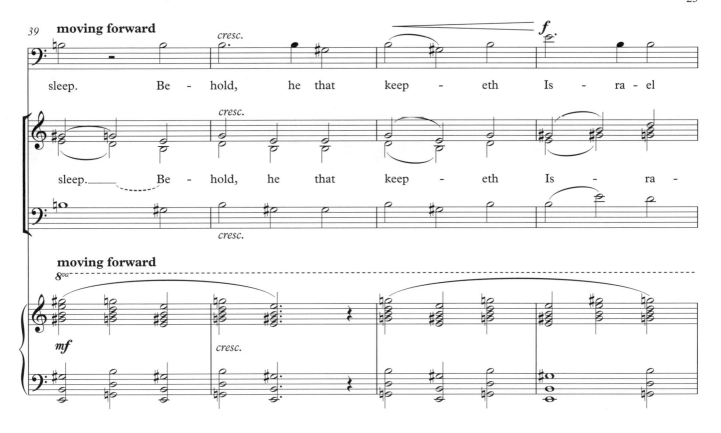

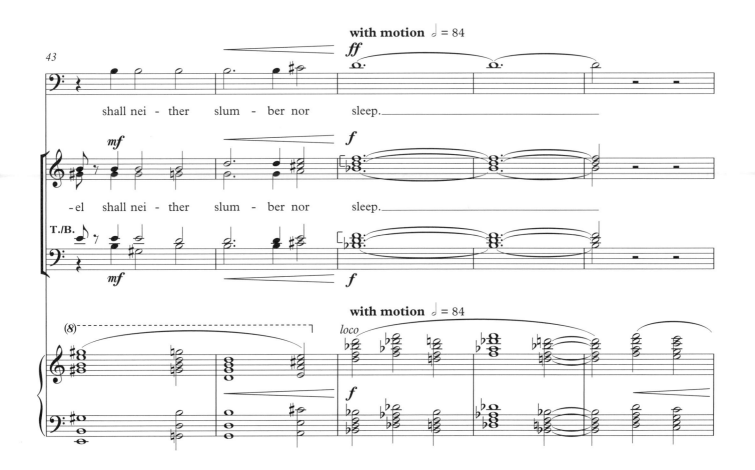

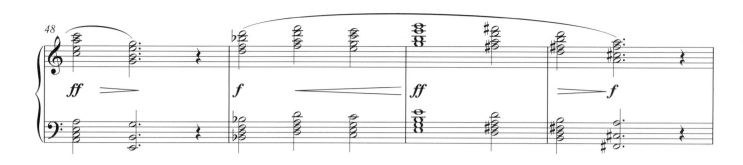

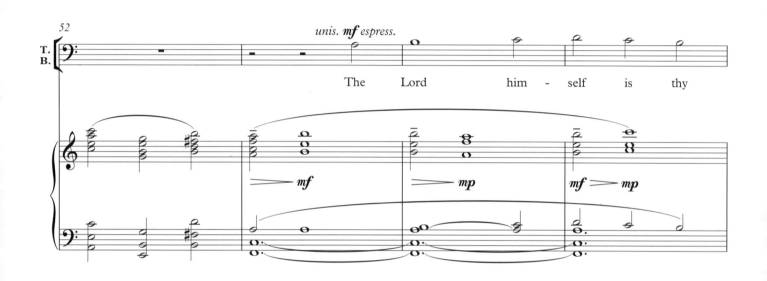

The Lord him-self is thy

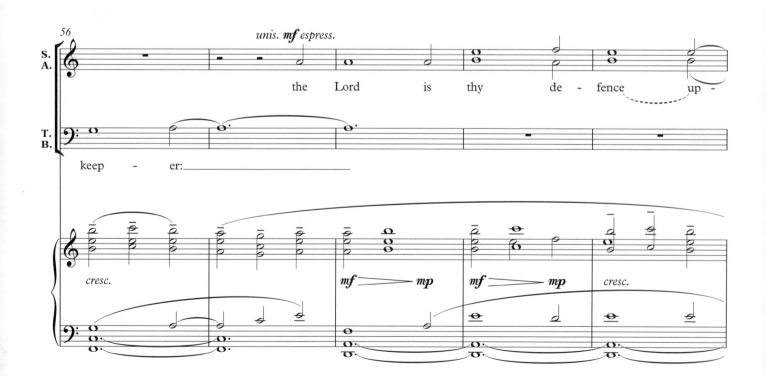

the Lord is thy de-fence up-

keep - er:

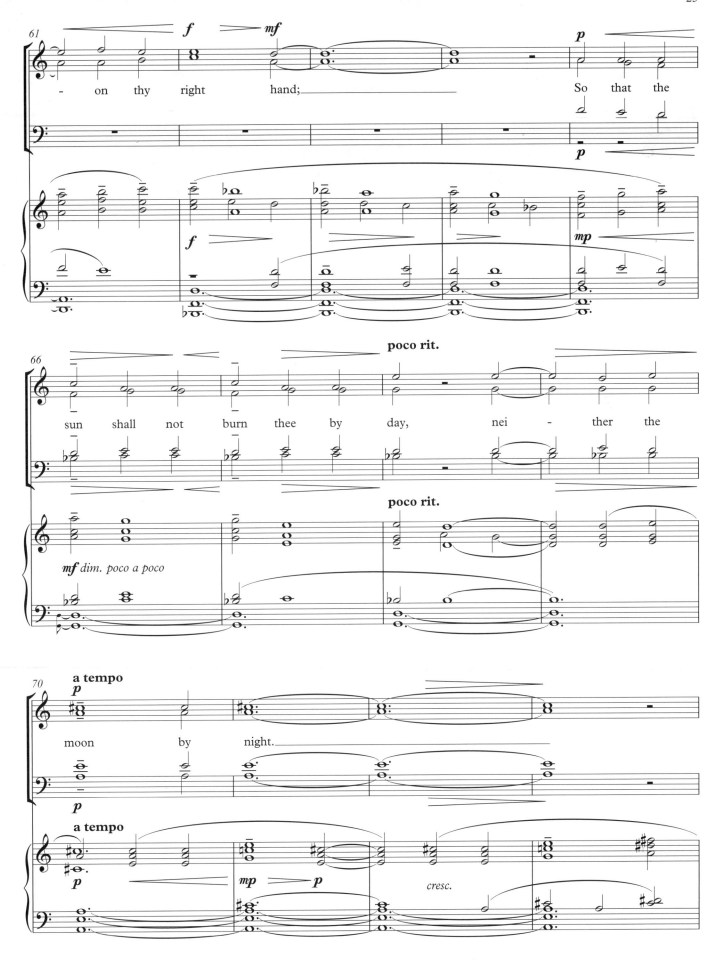

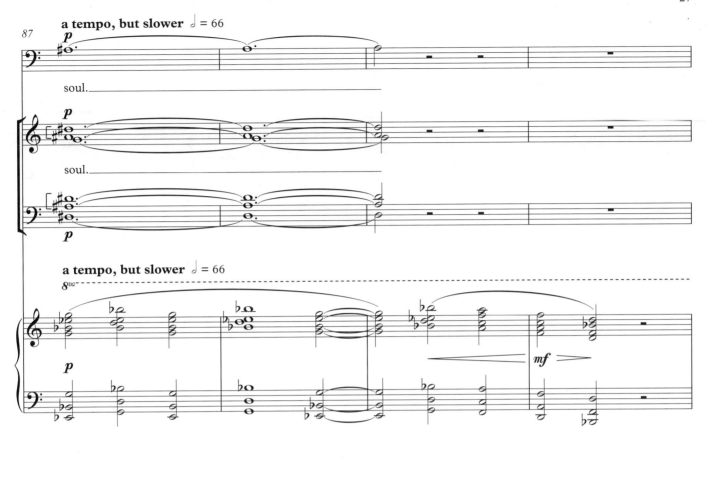

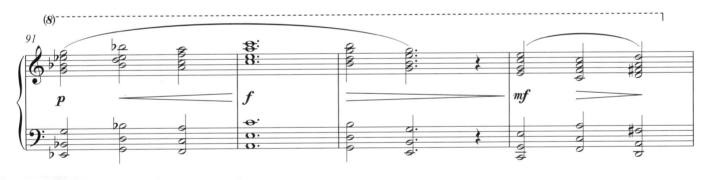

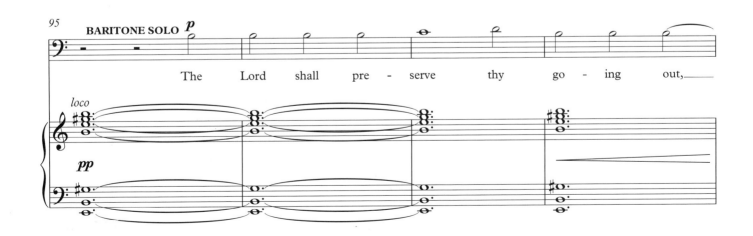

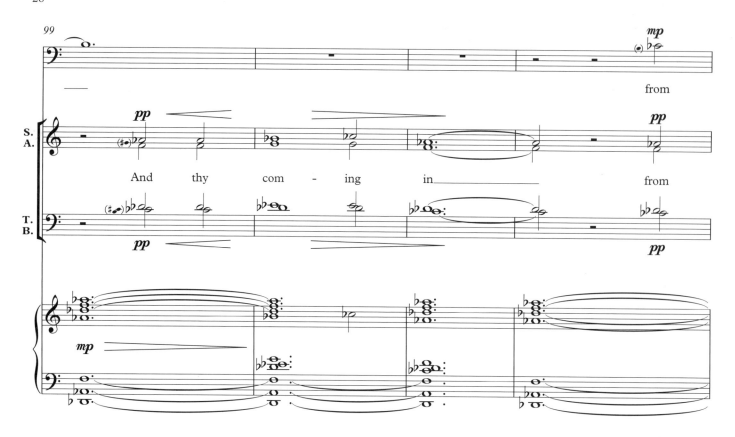

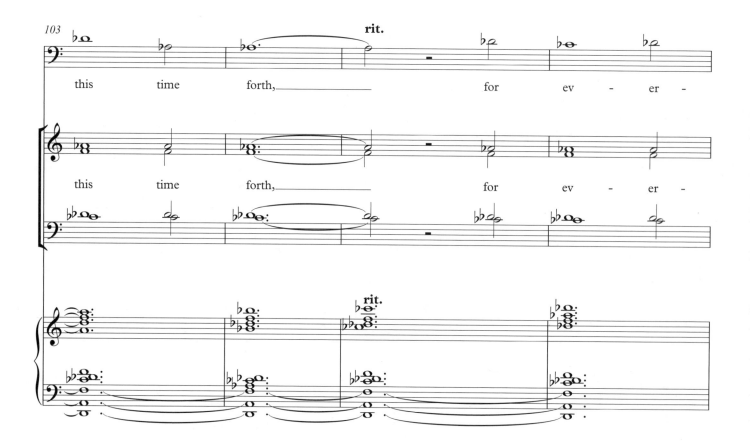

4. How lovely is thy dwelling place

Psalm 84:1–5, 7, adpt.

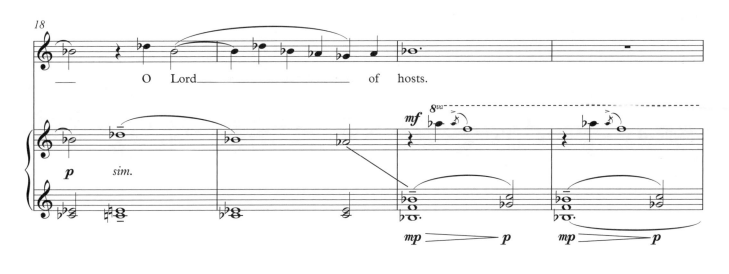

O Lord_____ of hosts.

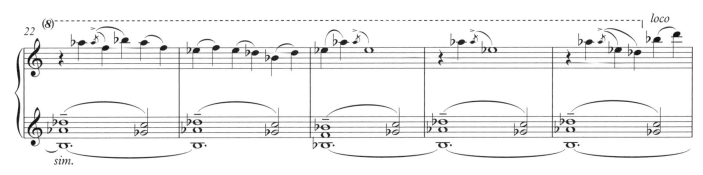

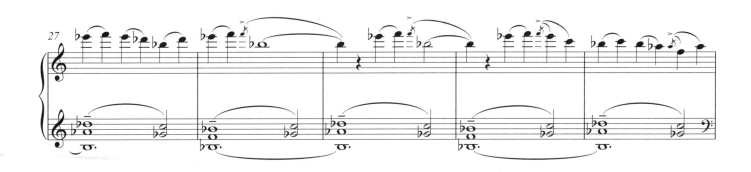

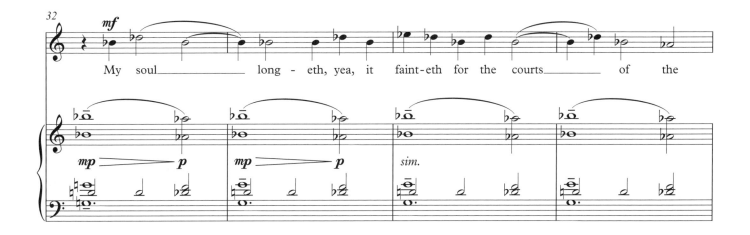

My soul_____ long - eth, yea, it faint-eth for the courts_____ of the

and my God.

34

5. O nata lux

10th-cent. Latin Hymn

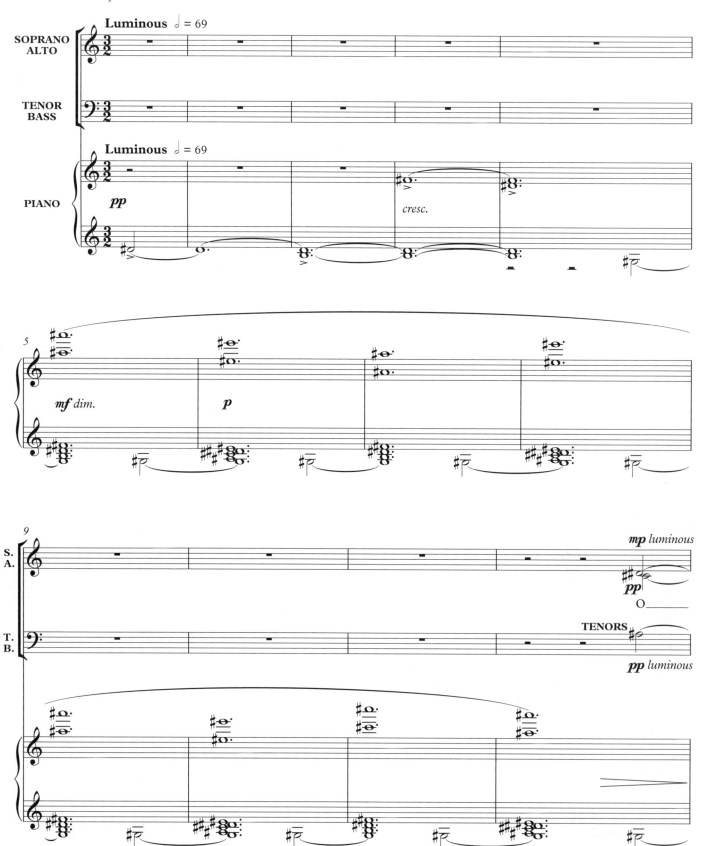

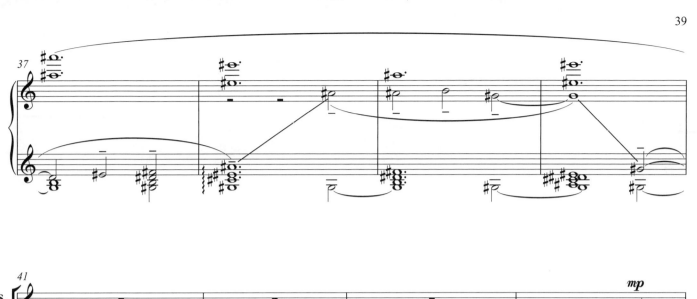

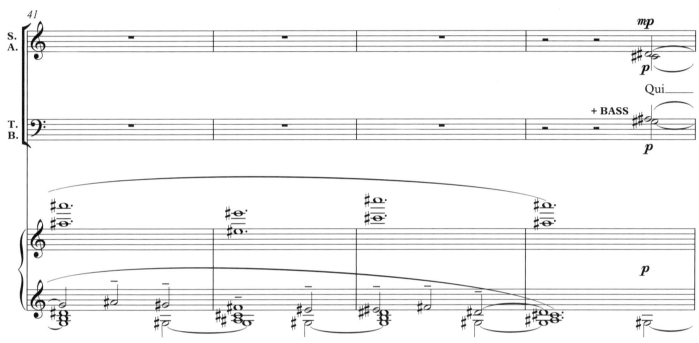

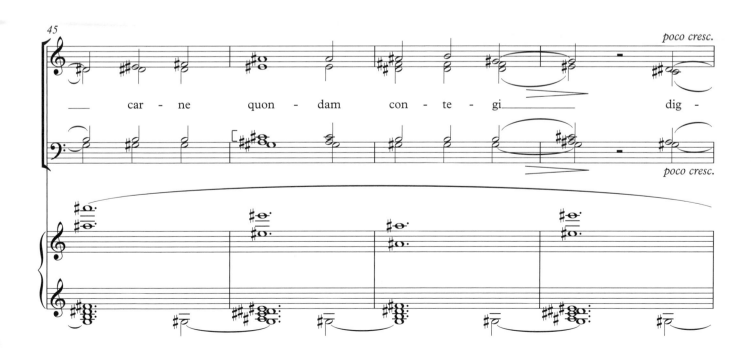

- su, re - demp - tor sae - cu - li.

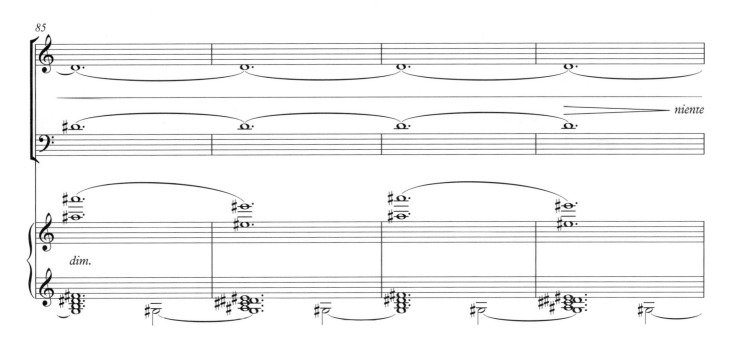

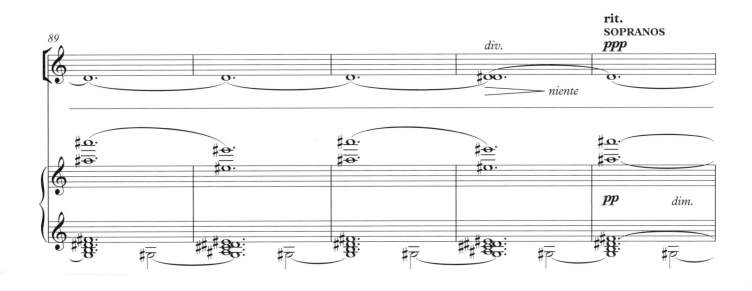

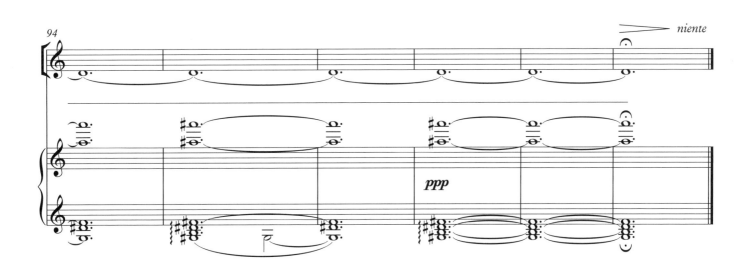

6. The Lord is my shepherd

Psalm 23, adpt.

He shall feed____ me in green pas - ture_____ and

lead me forth be - side the wa - ters of com - fort.____

He shall_____ con - vert my soul_____ and bring

____ me forth in the paths of____ right - eous - ness._____

7. I am the resurrection and the life— Requiem aeternum

John 11:25–6
Introit from Requiem

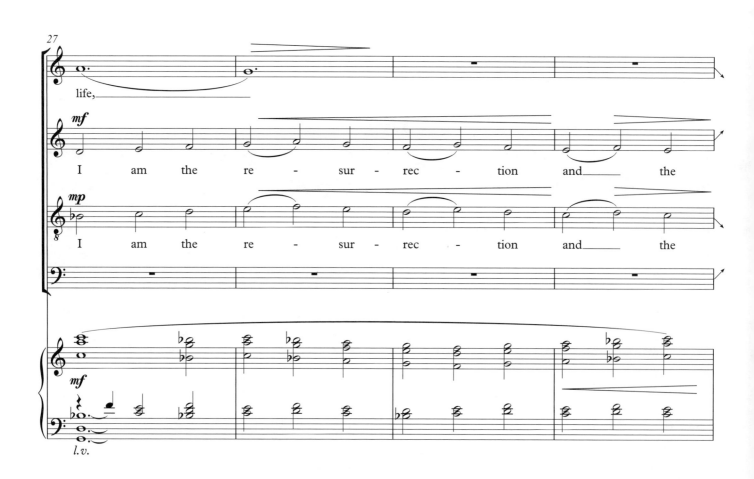

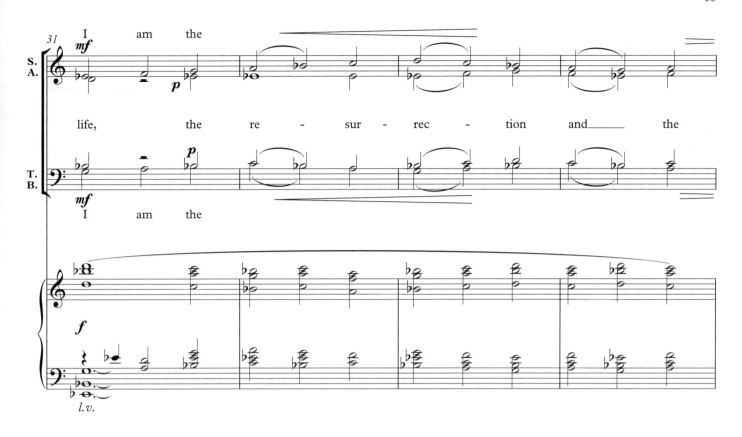

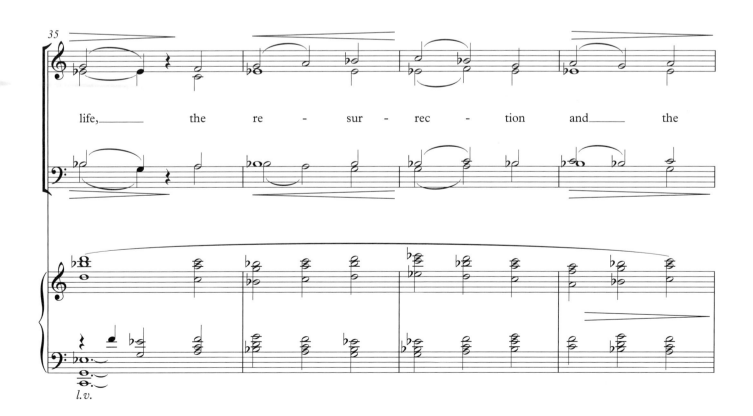

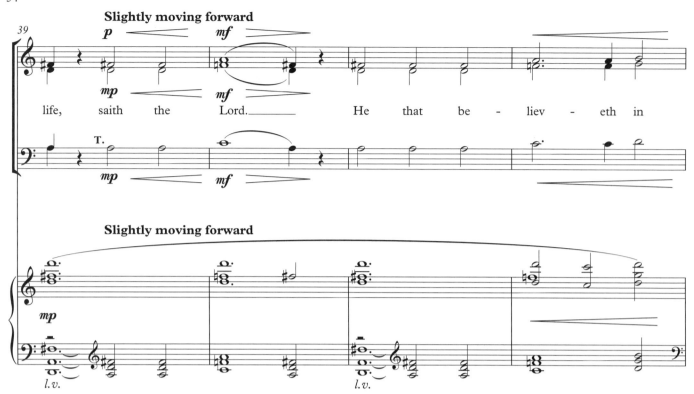

Slightly moving forward

life, saith the Lord._____ He that be - liev - eth in

Slightly moving forward

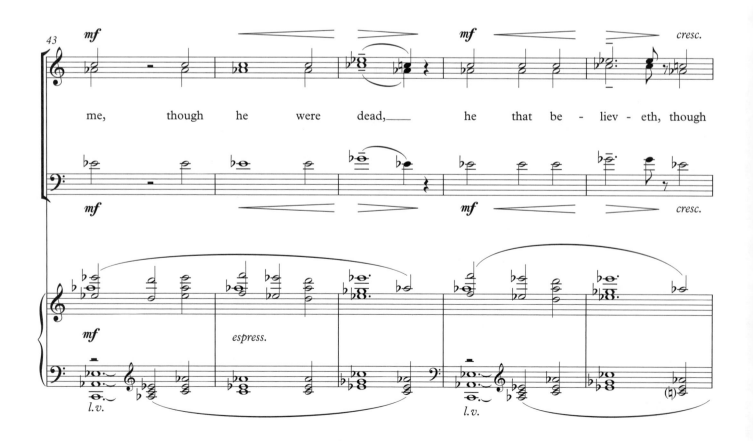

me, though he were dead,_____ he that be - liev - eth, though

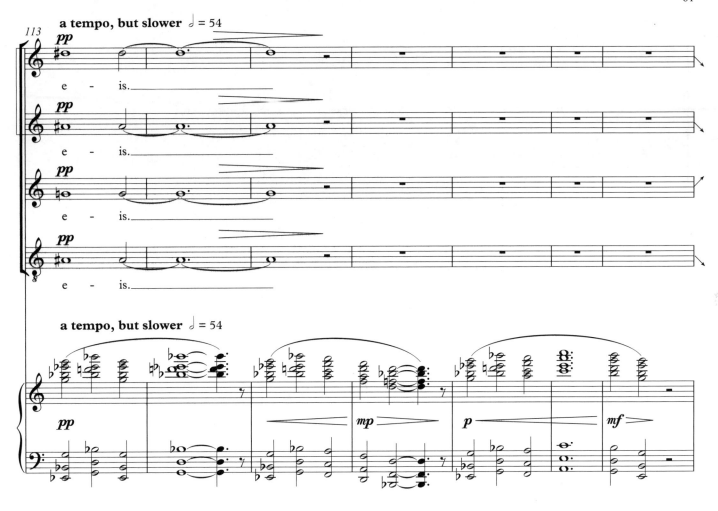

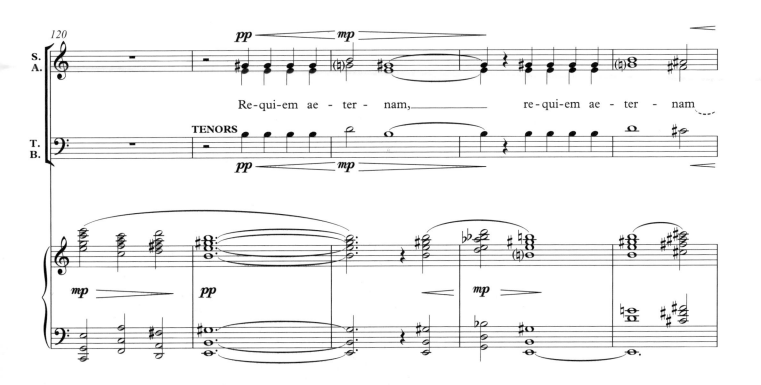

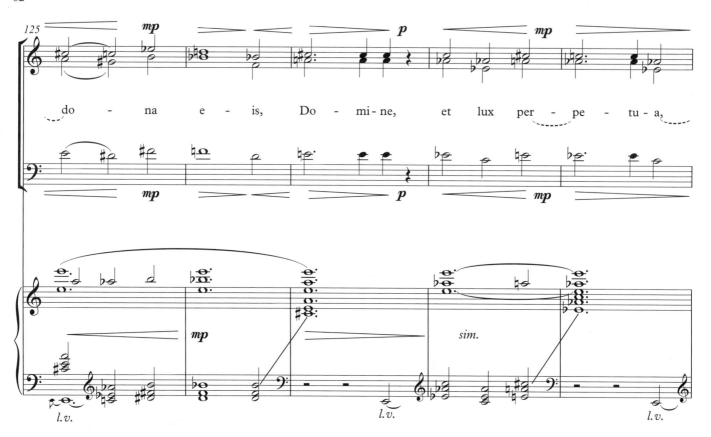

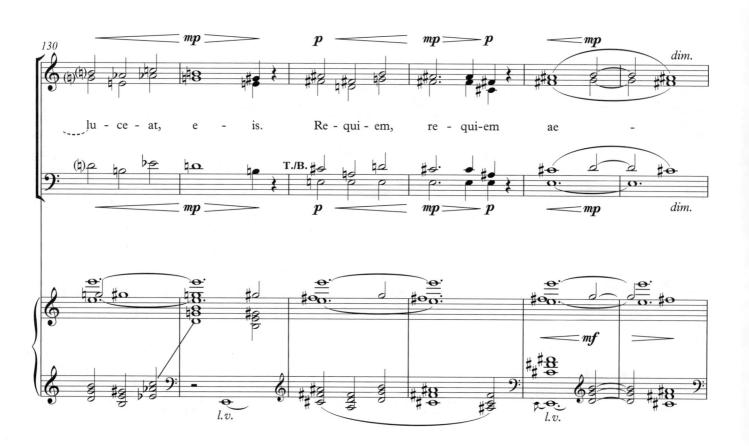

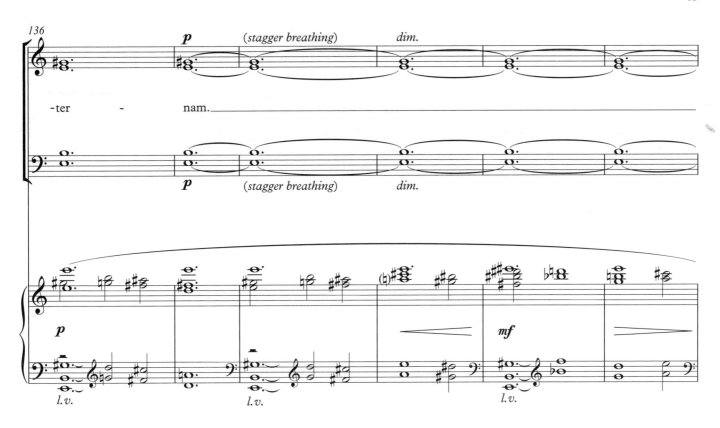

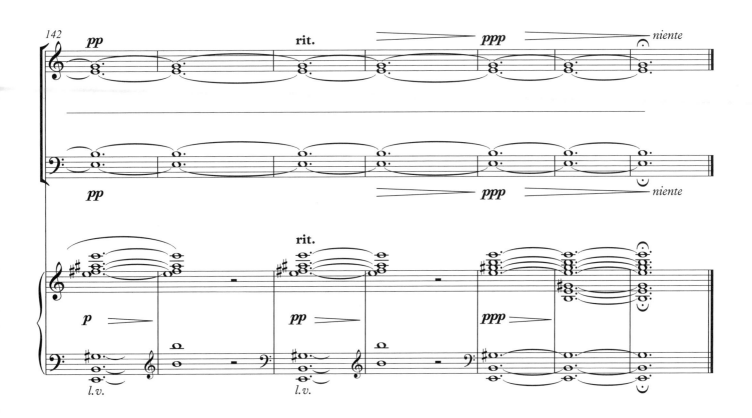